In-Decisisve

Malik E. White

Independently Published

ISBN: 9798842232000

Independently Published

ISBN 9798842232000

"Indecisiveness creates a masterpiece."

Table of Contents

The Blueprint to Happiness 9

It's About Time 10

Game Canceled 11

The Calm 12

Blossoming Satisfaction 13

Ever~lasting 14

Interlude I 15

Sometime Friends 16

Don't Take This Personal 17

Contra~Diction 18

Pain~ful 19

King's Downfall 20

Versus Mentality 21

My Reality 22

Edumacation 23

Sunshine 24

Losing Desire 25

Undeniable 26

My Non-Existence	27
Interlude II	28
ME	29
I Don't Know	30
I Can't Deal	31
Question's	34
If Only	35
In-Decisive	36
Introduction	40
Relationship	42
The Growing Tree	45
Purpose	49
Choose Wisely/No One is Perfect	51
Allow Yourself to Feel	53
Acceptance vs. Acknowledgement	54
Notes + Acknowledgements	56
A Message From The Author	57

The Blueprint to Happiness

I've been given the blueprint for happiness in its purest form.
Taking control of your destiny meant for you.
Finding a purpose that doesn't just benefit you.
Become an exclusive version of you.

I've been given the blueprint for happiness in its purest form.
Creating an understanding.
understanding physical life has its end.
Ending and eliminating all doubt placed upon oneself.

I've been given the blueprint for happiness in its purest form.

It's About Time

I am cluttered with emotions.
The mind contradicts the heart and yet I still try to remain open.

Missing the trueness of love I once received
Only to look back and question what true love really means.

Is it I who has been the reason for love's failure?
It seems like that, at least that's what all my ex's would tell ya.

For change doesn't always result in growth
But I continue to change and never know if it's for the better.

Game Canceled

Play with your emotions on your own time
For when you test mine
It becomes a war like back in '05
When I never took love serious and just played a game as mister nice guy

Play with your emotions on your own time
Always bring up old lies
Mixing them with a so called new life
Wearing shades so you can't realize

Play with your emotions on your own time
Thinking highly of your own mind
Bravo
But know you are not perfect but still want to call yourself divine.

[CANCELLATION COMPLETED]

The Calm

The calm before the storm unleashes a rain of worries.
Thinking to myself creates life's many version.
For calm is only good if you grow unto it.
Stuck in calmness -
Stuck comfortableness -
Not accustomed to change.

Tranquility is eating at me.
Like an athlete i pause before gametime
understanding the assignment given to me.
Not knowing if it is truly for me.
Swimming in calmness -
Bathing in comfortableness -
Surrounded by change.

Blossoming Satisfaction

For when life brings joy
Stars align
Dwelling in a place of humble divine

I have found my sanctuary
I have come to a halt
To adore and to be

A smile grows as the sun pours
Down its everlasting vibration
Of magnificent and historical feelings

I still grow but have accepted change
I have come terms with me

Satisfaction understands change
Change waters satisfaction

Now I blossom

Ever~lasting

Let's not limit what we can do
Let's not limit where our love can go

To infinity and beyond is where your kisses send me
In space I find myself when I'm in your presence

An everlasting feeling, controlling my happiness is the only way it is deserve

I just wanna give what you have given me
The life of joy
The belief of forever
The desire for

Everlasting. Limitless. True meaning of....

Interlude I

went from a boy to a man/
but i never said goodbye/
really had me wondering about the ribbon in the sky/
looking over yonder/
not ready to go up/
got so much to do/
gotta get my work up/
game changed when i lost a friend/
told myself things won't be the same again/
looking at life behind the horizon/
now i ain't got no worries, i'm vibing/
unc said my soul is anchored/
i got God on my side, he my anchor/
now i won't complain/
so many thoughts running through my mind/
tryna see who pulls the trigger when it's my time/
but until then imma let my shine/
gotta stay focused, gotta be on my grind.

Sometime Friends

Them sometime friends really know how to find they way back.
When I'm smiling, they there.
When I'm up in finance, they there.
When I'm hurting..........

Them sometime friends really know how to find they way back.
When they're hurting, they there.
When they're up in finance.........
When they're smiling......

Them sometime friends always know how to find they way back.
Never realizing the pain that they cause
The negativity that they place upon one's mind.

I am done with sometime friends

Don't Take This Personal

My personale takes on a persona of confidence
Loving on me like I'm different to a common sense
I ain't never meant
To hurt feelings

Contra~Diction

From afar I see the blessings of a beautiful sunrise.

Yet reminded of a brighter sunset.

To uphold gratefulness to its higher praise and yet still doubt life.

The contradiction of going left then right all to end up right back where I started.

Is it Deja Vu?

Is it Life's Karma?

Pain~ful

Pain remembers pain.
Forgetting the love that once lived in a place of warmth.
Yet hurt is the only thing that asks for a reaction.

Sadness.
Madness.
Depression.

Why can't I smile when I feel loved?
The feeling that once dwelled in my heart has lost its memory.
Dementia takes over my emotions and yet I only remember pain.
Pain remembers me and love forgets me.

King's Downfall

Sometimes i feel like a king.
Other times i feel as air.
Essential for everyone, but never taken care of.

For as life holds many lessons and many lessons hold values.
Learning and still failing becomes another setback.
Set me back to when I was a young boy without purpose.

Yes, i hurt too much.
Yes, i cry tears of sorrow - wiping them with a tissue of embarrassment.
Continuing to put myself in harm's way..

Am i loved?

Versus Mentality

Who am i to contradict my mind, neglecting and not accepting.

Not acknowledging something that's been bothering me from birth.

i was born to a world that was put against me that was made to damage my mental.

Maneuvering and dodging obstacles, but yet i stumble and fall.

Stuck

i sit and i watch the day go by.
The sun rise and sets The moon rises and stares

Contemplating the meaning of life.
Only to realize that...
Accepting
Acknowledging
My mental health was the only answer.

My Reality

I, Malik White, have accepted my reality for what it is.

I have fallen short too many times and hope for the best next.

Hoping

only

leads

to empty

faith and

I fall.

Edumacation

Growth of a mind continues to become blind to the knowledge of life yet taking on the emotions of crimes.

Sitting in a classroom not learning but memorizing asking a question "What does this have to do with my life"

Edumacation = Street Smarts + Book Smart

Sunshine

Who holds the sunshine?
Does it last for long or does it fade away?
Life in the sunshine can only be described as self-happiness.

As the sun rises, changes become popular.
Acceptance becomes its dive.
Love becomes the water.

When the sun sets,
the sun still holds its shine.
As a smile comes to those who cry.

There is more to a sunshine than its brightness.
There is more to a sunshine than its blindingness.
Sun shine only becomes sunshine with togetherness

Losing Desire

First step of admission.

I am broken.

My cry for help has fallen on deaf ears.
No one understands that the way I move or the way I write is my cry out.
I have accepted the fact that I am different.
Always tryna be perfect only not admitting or admiring my flaws.
My flaws have fallen on my death ears.
I am blinded by what people feel my future should be losing sight of what I DESIRE.

Undeniable

I have
left my
insecurities
control the
narrative
of my
life.
My focus
had misguided
me away from
the fight.
What else
do I
need to
do to
prove
that
I am
right?

My Non-Existence

Sometimes I feel like I don't exist.
Just a soulless body going through everyday motions.

Sometimes I feel like I'm the worst.
I always say I will be better and I continuously take two steps back without even trying.

How can I be me when I always feel "me" isn't good enough.

Am I ---
    a bad son?
    a bad friend?
    a bad brother?
    a bad me?

The world would be better if I didn't exist.
People wouldn't have to deal with me being in my feelings.
People wouldn't have to understand my broken soul.

Interlude II

am i on your mind/
i want you to embrace me
like i'm back from doing time/
it's my insecurities
got me thinking that you ain't feeling me/
tryna find affection
but affection be treating me differently/
is it time for me to move on/
it gets so hard so i hold on/
pushing you away when i don't know/
it's 2 different sides but it's a domino/

ME

How could it be that I couldn't explain
From MECK (1), the kid from tbe C
To be in need of a little therapy (2)
until I find myself on book 3
Confused about what I see
Only to see that all 3 were true versions of me.

I Don't Know

I've lost myself in the concept of becoming a better me.
I don't know if words could describe my life
Yet I fear to be seen in a movie scene only to discuss my life of
being an unforgettable character that should've starred me.

I Can't Deal

I woke up and picked violence, with my words though.
Time to speak truth, the unheard of.
I get sick and tired of seeing my people hurt.
You fear us because of the little power we gained
And now you kill us

Too much silence.

Not enough support.
I got this feeling like our lives are on life support.

Destined to die by a bullet to the head.
Nightmares as i watch my family weep,
Not comprehending why i'm dead.

Sad. Mad. Confused. Scared.
Growing up not knowing when my day and time is near.

When they killed those Kings and Queens in New York, they
killed me too
Do you truly understand the magnitude?

Can't even praise God without fear of getting S H O T.
I'm rambling while my feet are in shackles and i'm shaking
because my confidence is in shambles.

Justification, denied.
"Saving the White Race"
Is that how you really feel?
So a gun with a slur saves that.
All Lives Matter until separation happens.
I wanna cuss so bad but Grandma said let God do the talking.
Karma is on its way.
I'm afraid because people say " Save the white race"
Which translates to "Kill Malik or any other Black royalty"
Tired of closing my mouth. Tired of being the target.

If this is progress then I don't wanna know what digression is.

I send my prayers out to those families affected by such tragedies.
I send my prayers to every black individual.
I send my prayers

As I send prayers, I cry the tears of the slain.

I fight the pain of the hurt.

I

JUST

CAN'T

DEAL

Rest In Peace.

Question's

When will the world ever learn?
Complications creating exclamation at the end of violence
Shootings turning into lootings of anger and confusion.

Why live?
Questioning is life worth it if I live in fear.

If Only

If only I knew.....

I'm sorry for not being there.
I allowed my selfishness and fear to take control.
I didn't want to see you in your worst state.
I couldn't handle the pain and sorrow it would've took,
saving my eyes from the flood of a century.

If only I knew......

I would've been there to tell you how much I loved you.
I would've kissed your forehead and smiled.
Memories would have been made,
but yet I shied away.

I'm sorry Auntie. I'm sorry Mame. I'm sorry uncle.

If only I knew, I would have shown.

In-Decisive

Wanting to live has become a struggle.
I hurt.
The one person I was able to talk to........GONE.

I just want to be me.
I want to help.
How can I help if I always lose myself?

I've lost faith in me.

I don't even trust myself.

I sit in my car wishing someone would put me out of my misery.
My cry for help has yet to be seen.

I hate to smile at times.
I find joy in crying.

It is hard to show true emotions when those around you depend on what was once you -

Before the pain.
During the hurt.

I always blame myself.
I struggle because of me.
I lose people because of me.
I am not in control.

My reason: "I want to make others happy"
Disregarding my own happiness.

I continue to fall into depression - - - Ignoring my purpose.

Sheltered. Wimp. Weak Minded.
Names I've been called all because I've been through the unexplainable.

I am invisible until death.

I just want realization instead of sympathy for my in-decisive pain.

Words From The Heart

Introduction

I am who I am and that is because I grew. When I was younger, I used to look at life like it was an amusement park. It was never because of the symbolism or the attributes of an amusement park, it was because of the fun that you could have. Life was easy, a spoiled kid who got everything he wanted, a smart kid who excelled in his studies from kindergarten to eighth grade, and a semi athletic ability that was enough for me to play basketball at Rosecrans Park. That is beside the point, life was easy until I got a glimpse of the real world.

My grandpa would tell me to keep God first in everything you do. I wish I took that advice seriously at the time it was given. The one time I began to do things "my way" without God being the center of my decision things went left. unseen dangers found their way into my life. Still not even comfortable talking about such things.

This isn't about me though this about something totally bigger than me. When you come from where I came from, you learn a lot from many different people and so many undesirable yet interesting scenarios.

All I am trying to do is speak facts and don you with my truth and how I view life. Indecisive may be the word for my confusion but yet my confusion allows me to take the best of the best of life and yet weather the worst. This ain't for the mind, these are words from the heart.

Relationship

Right off the back, when you are young (high school), you don't truly know what love is. You might know what love is when it comes to family, but you don't know what it means to be in love with a significant other. Truth be told, you are in love with the idea of having someone to call your boyfriend or girlfriend.

Your first relationship is a practice test. It is rare that the one you find yourself with will become your wife or husband in the future. So, let's refer to a relationship like a non-paid internship. You are not getting the fullness of that other person, but you are gaining qualities and experience from this "internship". The internship can turn into a full-time job, but it is rare that it would happen. Sometimes you get a better offer from another job that, in the long run, would be better for you.

I'm not saying that it doesn't always work out because there is a possibility that it might workout. The only way the first becomes your last, you must be truly and fully dedicated to that person and vice versa. No shortcuts in this journey, it's going to be a long journey that is filled with roadblocks, trees of shade, hardships, and at the end there is a reward of truly understanding what being in love is.

My first relationship was somewhat like that. I honestly thought she was the one for me. You put what you can put in. I didn't have any experience, but she had. I had the hugest crush on her, literally would do anything for her even if I had to put her before my desires. I thought I knew what being in love was. I even said the three word phrases to her first: *I love you.* (Don't say it if you don't know what it truly means). A fourteen-year-old freshman, just taken away by the fact that I had a girlfriend. Not knowing we weren't with each other for true love, but rather with one another for the convenience of it, for the title of girlfriend and boyfriend.

There are certain things to expect from your first relationship and this is all from my personal experience. You should expect a lack of originality within it. Through your first relationship, people tend to build off someone else's relationship. This is where we would see #goals coming into play. This creates a huge flaw within that first relationship because you and your significant other are trying to be like someone else which strays from you being who you are. It just adds to the point of being with that person for the status of being taken.

I went about it in that way because I was just in the relationships, at one point, just to be in them. This hurt me because it caused me to be emotionally disabled. Those effects from my first relationship carried on in other relationships until now. I finally began to use that first relationship as a learning experience.

An exercise to do is to reflect on the very first relationship you had and ask questions. As you reflect, the answers will come. After you get your answers, find time for yourself and grow so that you become ready when it is time to get in another relationship. In this answer, be honest with yourself and true to yourself because it can only benefit you even more.

Questions that may be of use:

1. What was your main goal/reason in being in that relationship?
2. Were you open and willing to sacrifice for that person that you were in a relationship with?
3. Were there things that you wish you would have done differently or that the significant other would have done differently?
4. What did you take away about yourself from that first relationship? Did the positives out-weigh the negatives or vice versa?
5. How much did you grow from that relationship?

The Growing Tree

Growth is most noted when you begin to make or create some type of change that might progress you in your life journey. This type of change normally comes when something Jurassic happens within your life. Not saying if that is the way it happens for you, you are not strong, but a stronger and non-blinded individual will notice without a Jurassic event to come and bring about knowledge of change. I say knowledge of change just because it takes a dedicated person to act open the knowledge of change.

One of those changes can be what you value in life. Aimed at particularly this generation and younger, clout chasing is something a lot of these young individuals are doing. So many are consumed with the thoughts of how many friends or followers that they have on Instagram. Making that the focal point of how they would judge someone because of the likes that get on a picture or a video. I get it, you want to be seen and there is nothing wrong with wanting attention, but how would attention give you though. If you look at some of these millionaires or billionaires, some of you may not even know them and they are successful not because of the attention they get through Instagram or any other social media account they have (if they have one), rather because of their hard work and time management.

I'm not telling what to value or what should be important to you, what I am basically saying is prioritize the key important things. For example, my value is my spirituality to family and friends to my success. My list can go on and on, but I have a steady foundation with what I value in my life. When you think about it, what drives you to become better every single day? When you answer that question, you begin to establish the concept of having purpose.

Purpose doesn't come just by living, there must be a foundation under the purpose and some type of safety net to catch you. It makes what you are doing much sweeter.

What do you look at as your purpose in your life?

Once answering that question, you will begin to understand how growth through change will help you fulfill your purpose. For example, I feel like my purpose is mentoring those that are coming up under me. Knowing what my purpose is will allow me to move a certain way and make certain changes. When making the changes that are necessary, remember that all changes done in a positive manner are equal. It does not matter whether the change is great or small because you are making progress as well as the genuine effort.

You must be able to define certain situations in your life and that will come to progress. Look at everything that you have been in or a part of as a learning lesson. Take away something from whatever it is, but don't let it hinder your growth. We all fall guilty to it. We hold ourselves hostage from something that we, individually, could benefit from in the end. You must be willing to step out of the comfort zone that you have placed yourself in. Comfort zones are not necessarily a zone that we are placed in but rather a barrier that you build around yourself. They can be good for; How long will you benefit from it? It's like a shelter, you have the necessities and you really don't have to go anywhere. At some point, those things that you have in the shelter will begin to run low and since you are so "comfortable" in the shelter, you probably don't want to leave. The whole thing is that leaving that comfort zone that you have created for yourself can be the reason you may be able to succeed in life as you would want to.

Your tree will begin to bear fruit and continue growing. As you begin to grow you will be able to provide shade to those in need of it. Your growth will lead to success and then you will be in the position to help someone else meet their needs and be successful. This is what we call the give back stage. When these stars get big some do genuinely give back but others do it for an Instagram post. As you began to grow and began to further yourself in your aspirations, what is stopping you from being an influence.

People confuse these certain ideas of what being an influence is. If you are an influence, it is more about action than your popularity. It is this one saying that goes around, "What have you done for me lately?". As individuals we have to realize that our impact goes way beyond what we can imagine. Giving games to someone who is entering a certain chapter in their life and helping them navigate is being an influence. Carrying yourself to a high standard is an influence.

Purpose

The one important thing as people of this Earth that we struggle with is finding out what is our purpose in life. We often get it confused with our dreams or goals at some point. One can say their dream is to become an entrepreneur and own a billion-dollar company. Does that mean that is their purpose in life, no it is not. You see, purpose goes way deeper than just doing something you have always wanted to do. Purpose takes on the concept of your impact on society. This poses the question, *what can you do to better society or even those around you?*

With finding out your purpose there is this journey of self-growth which is explained a little in scenario 2. You must learn about what your strengths and weaknesses are. An exercise to do is write your weaknesses down on paper. Once you figure out what they are, begin to create a plan or an outline on what are things you may do to eliminate or at least minimize those weaknesses. Then act on it, try to eliminate those weaknesses off the list. Eliminating those weaknesses from the list will be your journey or a part of your journey.

After doing that you have to trust the process. You will begin to question certain things and want things to happen on your terms which is usually quicker than how it is supposed to happen. You must exhibit patience. Patience is the one thing that we people have a hard time showing. For each one of us individually to find our purpose we will need patience. The reason why patience is important is because it is rare that you will figure out your purpose on the first go around.

Choose Wisely/No One is Perfect

Your choices define who you are. Imagine just being judged based on your own personal choices. Would you be satisfied? Would you be disappointed? We as people continue to look at the generation of the future and tell them *I am only trying to help you so you don't make the same mistake that I made when I was your age*: depriving them of life. With life comes mistakes and bad choices at some point. NO ONE IS PERFECT.

Let's keep it real, the only way someone can actually learn about life and the consequences is to experience. I find myself telling everyone that I didn't know life or begin the journey in becoming who I am until I started college. I didn't have anyone hovering over me and questioning decisions I made. The only person I was truly answering to was myself. This held me responsible for actions that I would do whether they were bad or whether they were good. Become who you feel you should be.

It is this poster that would hang on my grandma's wall and now hangs from my head. "Live. Laugh. Love" was what it said.. How should you learn to love or be able to laugh and enjoy if you are not living; you really can't. You have to learn how to live according to your standards, not anyone else's standards. That comes with being you and becoming who you are meant to be in the end.

Now I am not saying go out and do whatever. Yes, you should think about what decisions you are going to make, but be able to grow from them. Something has to come out of this period of your life. You can't learn and not make some sort of progress in life.

Allow Yourself to Feel

Emotions are defined as a natural instinctive state of mind. Being so, there is a set difference between emotions and feelings. You can't have one without the other because feelings are the conscious experience of emotions. You can basically say without feelings there are no emotions. Now that is just an opinion or research aspect. Let's speak on more of a human level. Allow yourself to feel without regretting the way you feel. We sometimes sit there and instead of embracing our feelings or even voicing our feelings, we begin to deflect and keep to ourselves. This can cause depression and harm not just your mental state, but as well as your emotional state.

Speaking as a young black male, it can seem hard to feel or be in touch with your emotions. Generally, some ethnic backgrounds don't really teach or allow for you to express your feelings or emotions without being labeled as soft or the notion that you aren't able to handle life. It is alright to be vulnerable. Being able to express and not feel embarrassment is a strength of its own. Allow yourself to feel happiness, hurt, sadness. Then become familiar with the idea of healing. Your feelings don't define you, you define your feelings. Feel to heal.

Acceptance vs. Acknowledgement

"With preparation comes acceptance", a saying that has driven the second phase of my life. The journey of acceptance is not that of an easy one. I think a lot of times acceptance can be a good and bad thing. It has its goods because it allows you to move on. On the other hand, it can cause a stunt in your growth as well. A lot of time acknowledgement and acceptance becomes confused with one another.

You can accept things in your heart and fail to acknowledge them openly. I look at acknowledgement as the furtherance of acceptance. Over time, things have become a blur in everyday life. I feel as if full acceptance only comes when you learn to accept who you are. Once you have begun to accept who you are you begin to acknowledge your beauties and your flaws.

Each has its own journey that only you can dictate how they go.

Notes & Acknowledgements

The Blueprint to Happiness was the first poem written for this book

The *Interlude* poems were once freestyles

Words From The Heart Section was written over the course of two years (during the time I released my 1st and 2nd book)

In-Decisive (The title poem) was written during a time I found myself questioning my own life

To those who encouraged me to tap back in for this book. I acknowledge you

A Message From The Author

As I sit here and write this 3rd installment within my poetry book collection, I pray for everyone. Things have become tough in the world today and a lot of challenges have begun to rise. This poetry was written without having a single focal point. I wanted my thoughts to be free-spirited and began to take direction on its own. With exceptions for the "Interlude" poems, each poem stands on a premise of its own. Throughout writing this book I also came across certain personal challenges that prolonged getting it done. Those challenges are also sprinkled throughout the book as well. It is okay to be indecisive at times.

More Life. More Blessings.

www.ingramcontent.com/pod-product-compliance
Lightning Source LLC
LaVergne TN
LVHW052102160826
845678LV00015B/3321

* 9 7 9 8 8 4 2 2 3 2 0 0 0 *